NARWHALS

JESSIE ALKIRE

Checkerboard Library

An Imprint of Abdo Publishing
abdobooks.com

ABDOBOOKS.COM

Published by Abdo Publishing, a division of ABDO, PO Box 398166, Minneapolis, Minnesota 55439.

Printed in the United States of America, North Mankato, Minnesota
102018
012019

Design and Production: Mighty Media, Inc.
Editor: Liz Salzmann
Cover Photographs: Paul Nicklen/National Geographic Creative (front), Shutterstock (background pattern, front and back)
Interior Photographs: AP Images, pp. 9, 20; Doc White/Ardea.com, pp. 5, 15; Internet Archive Book Images/Flickr, p. 19; NOAA/OAR/OER, p. 25; SeaPics.com, p. 13; Shutterstock, pp. 7, 10–11, 17, 23, 26, 28, 29

Library of Congress Control Number: 2018948529

Publisher's Cataloging-in-Publication Data
Names: Alkire, Jessie, author.
Title: Narwhals / by Jessie Alkire.
Description: Minneapolis, Minnesota : Abdo Publishing, 2019 | Series: Arctic animals at risk | Includes online resources and index.
Identifiers: ISBN 9781532116988 (lib. bdg.) | ISBN 9781532159824 (ebook)
Subjects: LCSH: Narwhal--Juvenile literature. | Marine animals--Adaptation--Arctic regions--Juvenile literature. | Environmental protection--Arctic regions--Juvenile literature. | Habitat protection--Juvenile literature.
Classification: DDC 599.543--dc23

TABLE OF CONTENTS

UNICORN OF THE SEA

The icy waters of the Arctic Ocean are still. Suddenly, something sharp erupts out of the water. It is a long tusk. The tusk is attached to the head of a spotted whale. It's a narwhal!

The narwhal is a mysterious animal. It is famous for its tusk. In fact, the narwhal is often called the "**unicorn** of the sea." Rarely seen in the wild, narwhals spend most of their time under thick ice in the Arctic.

The narwhal submerges itself in the icy waters once again. It lets out a click, listening for the sound waves to bounce off nearby prey. Then the narwhal dives straight down into the darkness!

The narwhal dives hundreds of feet, moving at a steady pace. Soon the narwhal finds prey, sucks it into its mouth, and swallows it whole. Nearly ten minutes have passed, but the narwhal isn't tired. This is just another day for the unicorn of the sea!

Like all whales, narwhals are mammals, not fish.

CHAPTER 2

NARWHALS AT RISK

The narwhal belongs to the family Monodontidae. This family includes just one other species, the beluga whale. Narwhals live in the icy waters of the Arctic year-round. Their range covers the oceans near Canada, Greenland, Norway, and Russia. But the **habitat** of the narwhal is being threatened.

For about half the year, narwhals live under the cover of thick ice. This ice is rapidly **decreasing** due to climate change. Without ice, narwhals are fully exposed. This increases narwhals' risk of being killed by humans and animal predators such as **orcas**.

Warming temperatures in the Arctic also change the **distribution** of narwhals' prey. Narwhals have a very specific diet and likely won't

WHAT IS CLIMATE CHANGE?

Climate change is periodic change in Earth's weather patterns. In recent years, scientists have observed an increase in the rate of climate change. Most scientists agree this is due to humans burning **fossil fuels**. Burning fossil fuels produces **greenhouse gases** which trap heat in Earth's atmosphere. This has led to rising global temperatures.

be able to adjust to new prey. These factors have made narwhals one of the animals most **vulnerable** to climate change.

AWESOME APPEARANCE

Narwhals have spotted white and black skin on their backs and white undersides. As narwhals age, they turn whiter. Narwhals got their name from Norse sailors. These sailors thought the narwhal's skin looked like that of a drowned sailor. In Norse, *nar* means "**corpse**" and *hval* means "whale." So in Norse, *narwhal* means "corpse whale."

Narwhals have small heads, short snouts, and short flippers. This reduces the surface area of the narwhal's body so it can better retain heat. Narwhals also have a thick layer of blubber that keeps them warm. Blubber makes up one-third of a narwhal's weight!

A narwhal's tusk is a tooth that grows through the narwhal's skin. Narwhals have the roots of two teeth. They are next to each other above the mouth. In most males, one tooth grows into a tusk. The other tooth usually never develops, but in some cases it does. These narwhals would have two tusks. Females can develop tusks, but it is very rare.

Young narwhals are bluish gray or black and adults are gray. Old narwhals are almost completely white.

The outside of a narwhal's tusk is soft, while the inside is hard. The tusk has 10 million **nerve** endings. This helps narwhals sense their surroundings. A narwhal's tusk can break. If this happens, the tusk will repair itself.

Scientists aren't sure what the purpose of the narwhal tusk is. Some think the tusk size is used to determine the rank of male narwhals. These scientists' theory is that a longer tusk indicates a higher rank. Male narwhals may also use their tusks to fight and compete for mates.

Others believe the tusk is a sensory organ. This is because of the tusk's many **nerves**. The nerves connect to the narwhal's brain. The tusk could be used to detect sound, temperature, water pressure, and more.

Regardless of the tusk's uses, it is not necessary for survival. Female narwhals do not have tusks and successfully live without them. In fact, females usually live longer than males. Females also take on important responsibilities, such as carrying and raising calves.

Some narwhal tusks grow as long as 10 feet (3 m)!

NARWHAL RELATIONSHIPS

Like other whales, narwhals are social animals. They live in groups called pods. The size of a pod can range greatly. Some may number 15 to 20 narwhals, while other pods may have hundreds! Some pods have both males and females, while others are all-male or all-female.

Narwhals communicate with one another through various noises. They click, squeak, and whistle. Narwhals also make sounds underwater for **echolocation**. Echolocation is the process of using sound waves to determine an object's location. For a narwhal, this object is usually prey.

Male narwhals may also communicate with each other by crossing tusks. Some scientists think this could be a friendly greeting. Others think it is a move to compete for mates.

Narwhals start breeding when they are four to seven years old. Female narwhals give birth once every three years. Narwhals mate in the spring. **Pregnancies** last 14 to 16 months.

Narwhals usually give birth to one baby at a time. Narwhal babies are called calves. Calves are blue-gray at birth. They develop spots as they get older. Female narwhals nurse their calves for more than a year.

Narwhal calves are 5.2 feet (1.6 m) long and weigh 180 pounds (82 kg) at birth.

CHAPTER 5

NARWHAL MIGRATION

Narwhals travel around Arctic waters throughout the year. During the winter, they live under permanent sea ice. This ice forms thick sheets that float on top of the water. Over time, currents and wind push against the ice sheets and form cracks.

Like other sea mammals, narwhals need to surface occasionally to breathe air. When they are under ice, they get air through these cracks in the ice. Narwhals use **echolocation** to find cracks. They surface under the cracks to breathe.

In the spring and summer, Narwhals go to areas free of ice. This is usually near the coast. Narwhals use these areas for reproduction and raising calves. In the autumn, coastal areas often develop "fast ice." This is ice that is connected to the ocean floor or nearby land masses.

Fast ice does not have cracks for narwhals to breathe through. Narwhals can become trapped under fast ice and die. So, narwhals avoid this by leaving their summer **habitats** before fast ice has time to form. This usually occurs in September. They reach their winter habitats by November.

When narwhals migrate, a pod can grow to over one thousand individuals!

DEEP DIVES

Narwhals spend much of the winter hunting and eating prey. Narwhals have a very specific diet. Their most common prey is Greenland **halibut**. They will also eat cod, shrimp, and squid.

In order to hunt their prey, narwhals must dive deep in the ocean. Narwhals can dive up to 5,905 feet (1,800 m) deep. They can stay underwater for longer than 25 minutes!

Narwhals have special abilities that help them dive successfully. One is the ability to store oxygen in their bodies. When narwhals dive, they can't take in air. So, they have to store oxygen for use while diving. Narwhals can hold a lot of oxygen in their lungs, muscles, and blood.

Another ability that helps narwhals during dives is **echolocation**. The sun's light cannot travel very far into the ocean, so the sea's depths are completely dark. In this darkness, narwhals use echolocation to find fish and other prey. Narwhals make clicking sounds. Then they wait for the sound waves to bounce off an object. The sound echoes back to the narwhal. This helps narwhals detect where prey may be.

Narwhals can dive deeper than most marine animals.

Once the narwhal discovers its prey, it sucks the prey into its mouth. Then the narwhal swallows the prey whole. Sometimes, a narwhal may even eat rocks by mistake!

NARWHALS THREATENED

Historically, narwhals' largest threat has been humans. Hunters have killed narwhals for their meat, blubber, and tusks. However, the United States banned narwhal imports in 1972. Narwhals are still legally hunted by **indigenous** groups in Canada and Greenland. But researchers think this hunting has little effect on narwhal populations.

The main threat for narwhals today is climate change. The Arctic is warming much more quickly than in the past. Warmer temperatures change the behavior and **distribution** of fish. This could lead to reduced prey for narwhals. Narwhals only eat certain types of fish. Scientists think narwhals won't be able to change their diet.

Warmer temperatures also mean **decreasing** ice. This is causing marine animals to move into narwhal territory. It's possible that some of these creatures will compete with narwhals for food. Others, particularly **orcas**, hunt narwhals. With less sea ice for protection, narwhals could be easier for predators to find.

Indigenous people have hunted narwhals for thousands of years. Doing so is a tradition in many of these cultures.

Climate change also causes more **unpredictable** weather in the Arctic. A sudden drop in temperature or a wind shift can cause flash freezing. This is when the cracks in the ice sheets freeze over. Without the cracks, narwhals can't breathe. Flash freezing is usually temporary, but can last long enough for narwhals to **suffocate** and die.

Climate change is also causing more human contact with narwhals. Shipping and **cruise** ship companies are taking advantage of **decreasing** ice. They have started traveling through the Arctic. These ships cause pollution and can injure or kill narwhals.

Oil and gas companies are interested in offshore drilling in the Arctic. To try to find oil and gas, companies do **seismic** surveys. These surveys use air guns and explosions in the water.

The noise created by these activities interferes with narwhals' ability to use **echolocation** and to communicate. Seismic surveys can even cause hearing loss in narwhals. If a narwhal is unable to hear, it cannot find prey and will die. If companies do find gas or oil, drilling may then cause oil spills. There aren't any known methods to effectively clean up an oil spill in the Arctic.

Narwhals live for about 40 years.

CHAPTER 8

IMPORTANCE OF NARWHALS

Scientists think narwhals are the species that will be most affected by climate change. This is because narwhals are creatures of habit. Besides having a specific diet, they also have a low reproduction rate. They may not be able to have enough calves to make up for population losses.

Narwhals are also important to other Arctic animals. Without narwhals, the Arctic ecosystem could be thrown out of balance. The populations of narwhals' prey species could increase. And the populations of barnacles and other creatures that live on the skin of narwhals could decline.

Indigenous people in Canada and Greenland would also be affected by the loss of narwhals. Narwhal hunting is part of the **culture** of these groups. Some still make a living hunting narwhals.

Narwhal tusk imports are banned in many countries. In countries where tusk sales are allowed, one tusk can sell for thousands of dollars.

SAVING NARWHALS

Narwhals are so rarely seen that scientists aren't sure how many narwhals there are. Estimates by different organizations range from 25,000 to 120,000. In 2012, the International Union for the Conservation of Nature (IUCN) listed narwhals as Near Threatened. This means they were threatened with extinction. However, the IUCN changed the narwhal's **status** to Least Concern in 2017. This means it is not considered to be as close to extinction as previously believed.

Many scientists and conservation groups continue to work to save narwhals. An important part of this work is trying to learn more about narwhals' lives. Researchers

IUCN

The International Union for the Conservation of Nature is a global authority on the status of wildlife. It collects scientific data and experts' studies to determine the status of a species. Then, governments and conservation organizations use this information to make decisions about species protection.

Many images and studies about narwhals have come from biologist Kristin Laidre. Her work has focused on narwhals' diet, diving, and migration.

continue to develop methods for studying narwhals. These experts hope that more information will help them find ways to save narwhals.

American biologist Kristin Laidre is a leading expert on narwhals. Laidre works with **indigenous** hunters in Greenland to study narwhals. She studies narwhal carcasses. Laidre also attaches transmitters to narwhals. This helps Laidre track the animals and their migration habits.

World Wildlife Fund Canada (WWF Canada) is working on a similar project. In 2011 and 2012, WWF Canada workers attached tags to narwhals near North Baffin Island. The tags can be tracked by

野生動物の保護
Protection of wildlife

satellite. This helps researchers track the narwhals' movements and feeding and reproductive habits. Researchers hope these studies will help us better understand the **unicorn** of the sea.

Other groups focus on laws and regulations to help narwhals. Hunting of narwhals is only legal for **indigenous** groups in Canada and Greenland. Still, conservation groups think there should be stronger hunting regulations. As a result, limits on how many narwhals can be hunted each year have been developed. Further bans on imports and exports of narwhal tusks may be explored as well.

The International Whaling Commission (IWC) is a whale regulation organization. It is in charge of regulating hunting and other issues affecting whales. The World Wildlife Fund (WWF) is working with the IWC to create regulations on climate change, oil drilling, and shipping.

Conservation groups like WWF, Oceana, and the TerraMar Project also raise awareness about climate change's effects on marine animals. With a combination of education, awareness, and laws, people can save narwhals!

People are very interested in the mysterious narwhal. Narwhals are often featured in marine museums so people can learn more about them.

NARWHAL
FACT SHEET

SCIENTIFIC NAME:
Monodon monoceros

LENGTH: 13 to 20 feet (4 to 6 m)

WEIGHT: 1.5 tons (1.4 t)

DIET: carnivore

AVERAGE LIFESPAN IN THE WILD: 40 years

IUCN STATUS:
Least Concern

WHAT CAN YOU DO?

You can take action to help narwhals and other Arctic animals at risk!

- Give money to or volunteer for wildlife conservation and research organizations that work to help narwhals. These include Oceana, World Wildlife Fund, and the TerraMar Project.
- Write to local lawmakers asking them to support policies that protect narwhals. These policies include laws that limit **greenhouse gas** emissions.
- Tell your friends and family about climate change and how it affects Arctic wildlife such as narwhals.
- Reduce your individual use of **fossil fuels** by choosing to bike, walk, or take the bus instead of riding in a car.

GLOSSARY

corpse—a dead body.

cruise—a vacation on a ship.

culture—the customs, arts, and tools of a nation or a people at a certain time.

decrease—to make or become less, smaller, or fewer.

distribution—the area over which a particular thing is spread.

echolocation—a process for locating distant or unseen objects using sound waves.

fossil fuel—a fuel formed in the earth from the remains of plants or animals. Coal, oil, and natural gas are fossil fuels.

greenhouse gas—a gas, such as carbon dioxide, that traps heat in Earth's atmosphere.

habitat—a place where a living thing is naturally found.

halibut—a large fish that lives in the Atlantic and Pacific Oceans that is often eaten as food.

indigenous—native to a certain place.

nerve—a bundle of fibers carrying messages between the brain, the spinal cord, and other body parts.

orca—a black-and-white whale species. Orcas are also called killer whales.

pregnancy—the condition of having one or more babies growing within the body.

satellite—a manufactured object that orbits Earth. It relays scientific information back to Earth.

seismic—of or relating to vibrations in the earth.

status—a state or a condition.

suffocate—to die from lack of oxygen.

unicorn—an imaginary animal that looks like a horse with one horn growing out of its forehead.

unpredictable—unable to be guessed or declared in advance.

vulnerable—able to be hurt or attacked. An animal has a vulnerable status when it is likely to become endangered.

ONLINE RESOURCES

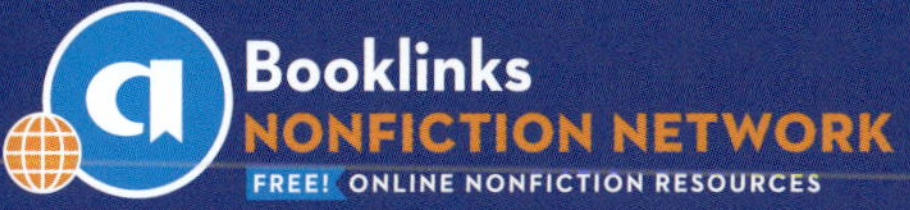

To learn more about narwhals, visit abdobooklinks.com. These links are routinely monitored and updated to provide the most current information available.

INDEX